ANDI'S BIRTHDAY

WRITTEN BY
CATHERINE BARELA

To order additional copies of this book, contact:
Xlibris
844-714-8691
www.Xlibris.com
Orders@Xlibris.com

ISBN: Softcover   978-1-6698-1787-1
        EBook   978-1-6698-1786-4

Print information available on the last page

Rev. date: 03/25/2022

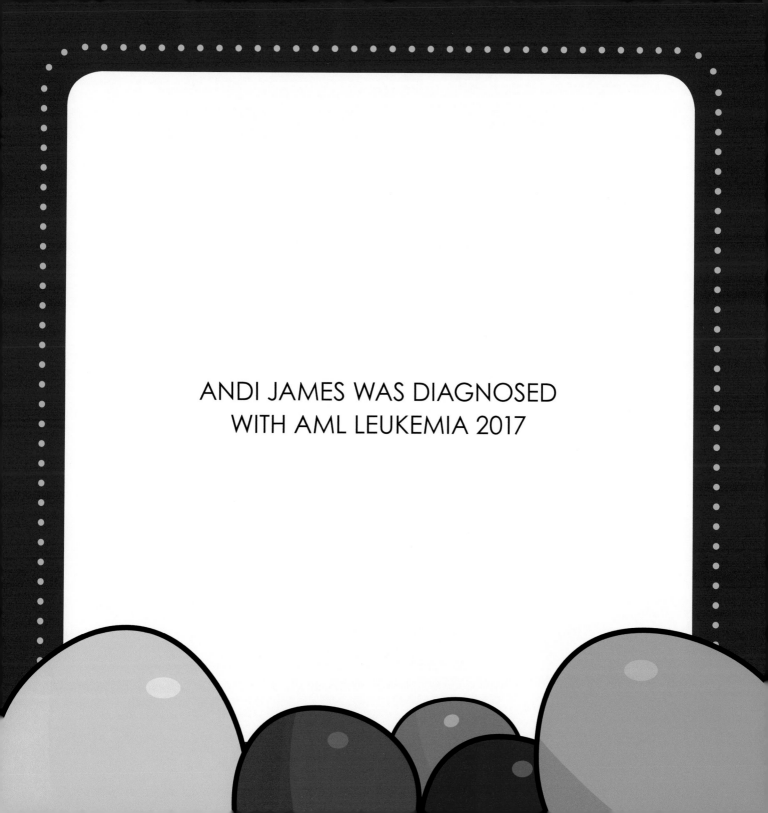

ANDI JAMES WAS DIAGNOSED
WITH AML LEUKEMIA 2017

THIS BOOK IS DEDICATED TO Andi's PARENTS: LANI (MOM), ADRIAN (DADDY), AND MY TWO SISTERS ANNA (18) AND PHOENIX (6)

HI I'M ANDI!

I'M LEAVING THE HOSPITAL TODAY!

AFTER SIX WEEKS OF TREATMENT HERE, I'M EXCITED TO FINALLY be Going HOME

TO PLAY WITH MY SISTER PHOENIX!

This is my sister Phoenix (Andi) giggle!

6

I'M SO HAPPY TO BE HOME FOR MY BIRTHDAY!!!

I GET TO PLAY IN MY ROOM WITH ALL MY TOYS!

This is my puppy Bogey (Boyee) I can't say Bogey This is my grandma's house (mum mum's house).

Mum Mum is my best friend and I'm the love of her life!

I love mum mum!

Today is my Birthday

Andi's Birthday

This is my family Mommy, dada, Anna and
Phoenix I love you!

Thank you for my Birthday!

This is my Birthday Dress.

Today is my Birthday!

My Birthday!

Andi's Birthday!

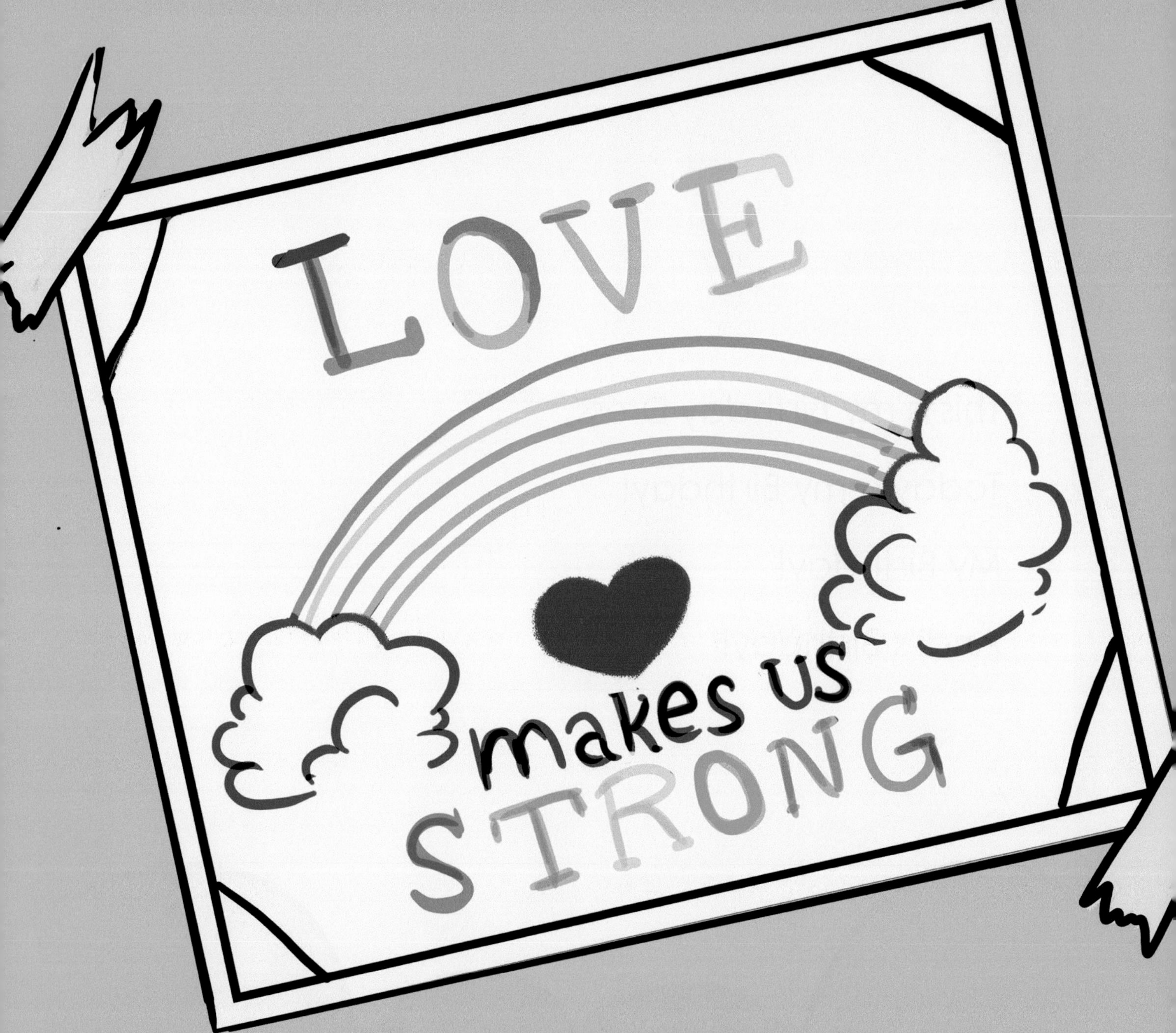
LOVE
makes us
STRONG

Love Makes me Strong!

If only Love could cure!

I am Strong –Andi strong!

I am Brave!

I am Loved!

And I am back in the Hospital!

Hugs and Kisses to my family!
Love Andi

Childhood cancer is real!

For those who have not lived in the world of cancer, consider yourself fortunate!

It takes strength, endurance, love, patients, and courage. It is a rollercoaster of emotions for the family!

Andi was stronger and braver than any toddler I've ever known!

She will always be remembered for her remarkable self. We will always love you Andi and we wish you a million more birthday's in heaven!

Love, Mum Mum